wondrous love

DEVOTIONS FOR LENT 2020

AUGSBURG FORTRESS

Minneapolis

WONDROUS LOVE
Devotions for Lent 2020

pISBN 978-1-5064-6149-6
eISBN 978-1-5064-6441-1

Writers: Paul E. Hoffman (February 26–March 3 and April 9–11), Barbara Melosh (March 4–10), Ron Valadez (March 11–17), Shelly Satran (March 18–23), Jennifer Phelps (March 24–April 1), Harvard Stephens Jr. (April 2–8)

Editor: Laurie J. Hanson
Cover image: Waterfall in the Krka National Park, Croatia, Europe/robertharding/SuperStock
Cover design: Laurie Ingram
Interior design: Eileen Engebretson
Typesetting: Emily Wyland

Manufactured in the U.S.A.

20 19   1 2 3 4 5 6 7 8 9 10

Welcome

What wondrous love Jesus shows for us and the world in his journey from baptism to the empty tomb! In Matthew (the gospel focus for 2020, year A in the Revised Common Lectionary) Jesus predicts that he will be betrayed, arrested, abandoned, and put to death, yet he continues on to Jerusalem and the cross. This wondrous love accompanies, guides, and empowers us on our journeys toward Easter's baptismal renewal in Christ. It inspires us to sing, serve, and share God's love with others.

Wondrous Love provides a devotion for each day from Ash Wednesday to the Vigil of Easter (traditionally known as Holy Saturday). Devotions begin with an evocative image and a brief passage from the Gospel of Matthew. The writers then bring their unique voices and pastoral wisdom to the Matthew texts with quotations to ponder, reflections, and prayers.

May God's wondrous love be with you during this Lenten season as you walk with Jesus and live into your baptism.

What wondrous love is this, O my soul, O my soul!
What wondrous love is this, O my soul!
What wondrous love is this that caused the Lord of bliss
to bear the dreadful curse for my soul, for my soul,
to bear the dreadful curse for my soul?
—North American folk hymn,
   "What wondrous love is this," ELW 666, st. 1

February 26 / Ash Wednesday

Matthew 3:1-2, 5-6

In those days John the Baptist appeared in the wilderness of Judea, proclaiming, "Repent, for the kingdom of heaven has come near." . . . Then the people of Jerusalem and all Judea were going out to him, and all the region along the Jordan, and they were baptized by him in the river Jordan, confessing their sins.

To ponder

Savior, when in dust to you low we bow in homage due;
when, repentant, to the skies scarce we lift our weeping eyes;
oh, by all your pains and woe suffered once for us below,
bending from your throne on high, hear our penitential cry!
—Robert Grant, "Savior, when in dust to you," ELW 601, st. 1

Who we are

Ashes are what's left when the thing itself is gone. Though we don't like to think about it, one day we will be gone. And sooner or later after that day, we will return to the ashy dust from which God made us. Today, more than any other in the church year, is the day to remember and be blessed by the truth about who we are. Sometime today you may stand before another whose words, "Remember that you are dust . . . ," will be punctuated by a cross upon your forehead.

Matthew reminds us of similar words and gestures from John the Baptist. Of special significance are the two words *repent* and *confess*. To repent means to "turn around." Good Ash Wednesday advice. Turn around from our illusion of self-sufficiency and face God, which means facing the truth of who we are. This is a day to turn around and confess that we get it: one day we will once again be ashes.

Ash Wednesday also reminds us of the promise of this Lenten journey. We are moving toward Easter's baptismal renewal in Christ. There is our hope. The one who made us from dust has remade us in the refreshing stream of baptismal waters—and makes us new every day.

Prayer

God, we stand before you in humility and gratitude. Thank you for the promise of baptism, assuring us that, by your grace, we who were made from dust and will return to ashes have nothing to fear. You will make us new. Amen.

Matthew 3:11, 13

[John said,] "I baptize you with water for repentance, but one who is more powerful than I is coming after me; I am not worthy to carry his sandals. He will baptize you with the Holy Spirit and fire. . . ." Then Jesus came from Galilee to John at the Jordan, to be baptized by him.

To ponder

Christ is baptized, not to be made holy by the water, but to make the water holy. —Maximus of Turin, "Sermo 100"

Water is thicker than blood

All water is connected. Just think of it: in a sense every drop of water on earth ran over the body of Jesus as John baptized him. I think Jesus would love it if we could remember that all people are connected too. Water is thicker than blood.

If you attended Ash Wednesday worship, you probably heard about fasting, one of the disciplines of Lent. Fasting is choosing to go without something—alcohol or chocolate, swearing or trash-talking our neighbor. We are all connected to Christ, and by our baptism into Christ we are connected to one another. So perhaps a fast of a more substantial nature is in order. What might it be like for God's people to fast from discrimination and prejudice? What if we fasted from our usual way of thinking about others who are not like us, and prayed for God's wisdom in seeing all people as beloved children of God?

"I am not worthy." John's words could become our own this Lent, not in a self-denigrating way, but in a way suggesting that I am no more worthy than any other person on earth, than any other person touched by and blessed by the waters that ran over Jesus. In that, we may find a new sense of the fire of the Spirit burning within us.

Prayer

Lord Jesus, we praise you for your baptism that makes all water holy and calls us to new life. Help us by your grace to see the value in every human being, and to understand more fully that we are all siblings with one another and with you. Amen.

February 28

Matthew 3:16-17

When Jesus had been baptized, just as he came up from the water, suddenly the heavens were opened to him and he saw the Spirit of God descending like a dove and alighting on him. And a voice from heaven said, "This is my Son, the Beloved, with whom I am well pleased."

To ponder

When you pass through the waters, I will be with you;
and through the rivers, they shall not overwhelm you.
—Isaiah 43:2

Beloved

Water is a strange and wonderful thing. It can both kill and save, bring destruction and heal. The right amount is essential for earth's life and growth—and ours too. Too little water and we shrivel and die. Too much and we find ourselves overwhelmed.

The promise of the prophet Isaiah gains a new perspective in the baptism of Jesus. We see Jesus named "Beloved," one in whom God is well pleased. Not an overwhelming message at all; rather, one we all long to hear.

These days between ashes and Easter provide the Christian community with an opportunity to prepare for that magnificent baptismal passage of Jesus from death to life. The Greek word for Easter, *pascha*, means "passage." It evokes so many different passages for us: the Israelites' passage from slavery to freedom, our own passage from sin to forgiveness, Jesus' passage from death to life, and—maybe most poignant of all—the passage from despair to hope.

God knows just the right amount of water: enough for us to pass through; not so much as to overwhelm. In that sweet spot of baptismal washing, God reminds us that we are beloved.

Prayer

Gracious God, we give thanks for the gift of baptism in which you name us, claim us, and call us beloved. What wondrous love is this! Amen.

Matthew 4:1-4

Then Jesus was led up by the Spirit into the wilderness to be tempted by the devil. He fasted forty days and forty nights, and afterwards he was famished. The tempter came and said to him, "If you are the Son of God, command these stones to become loaves of bread." But he answered, "It is written, 'One does not live by bread alone, but by every word that comes from the mouth of God.'"

To ponder

Guide me ever, great Redeemer,
pilgrim through this barren land.
I am weak, but you are mighty;
hold me with your pow'rful hand.
Bread of heaven, bread of heaven,

feed me now and evermore.
feed me now and evermore.
—William Williams,
   "Guide me ever, great Redeemer," ELW 618, st. 1

Connected to the larger story

Jesus' responses to the devil in Matthew all allude to Israel's desert wandering. The dust of Ash Wednesday is now the dust of the desert. Even Jesus' story is connected to a larger story.

We too are connected to this larger story in scripture. How have we been tempted? How have we survived temptation—or not? In what ways have we been guided by the great Redeemer? When have we felt God's powerful hand, or feasted on the bread of heaven?

Making these connections to scripture's larger story leads us to wisdom and strength for our journey. In the deepest hours of temptation and abandonment, we are not alone. We are held in the powerful hand of one who made a similar journey and makes us part of something bigger than ourselves. We belong to a people who have wandered through the desert and fed on the bread of heaven. Our community of faith supports us in our journey. We are part of a weekly gathering around a Word more substantial than bread alone. God nurtures us with the bread and cup given by the One who himself walked our barren land.

Prayer

Guide us ever, great Redeemer. Lead us by your hand and help us to remember with gratitude that you are always with us. Amen.

March 1 / Lent 1

Matthew 4:5-7

Then the devil took [Jesus] to the holy city and placed him on the pinnacle of the temple, saying to him, "If you are the Son of God, throw yourself down. . . ." Jesus said to him, "Again it is written, 'Do not put the Lord your God to the test.'"

To ponder

[The Lord] said to me, "My grace is sufficient for you, for power is made perfect in weakness." —2 Corinthians 12:9

A different kind of power

Before his ministry even gets out of the gate properly, Jesus is already at work exercising his power. But it is a different kind of power. We see it at work in his resistance to the devil: "Do not put the Lord your God to the test." Jesus' power is a power made perfect in weakness.

From the pinnacle of the holiest building in the holiest city, Satan throws down the gauntlet. But Jesus isn't playing that game. He has no interest in showing off his divine powers or even testing them. He builds on a new foundation. It is a foundation of wondrous love that to human eyes often looks like weakness. His is a love that is selfless and seeks to serve.

We are a people who dwell in skyscrapers, both real and metaphorical. We love it at the top. Satan thought he could catch Christ in that trap. But Jesus begins his ministry, still dripping with the waters of baptism, as a citizen of a new creation. To the devil and to the cosmos he sends a message loud and clear: *The power of the God who sent me is the power of wondrous love. It has nothing to do with showy affectations of worldly power. I have come among you as one who serves.*

Prayer

Lord Jesus Christ, strip us of all false notions of power. Teach us to love the world as you love it, with a generous share of selfless compassion—the foundation for true power. Amen.

Matthew 4:8-11

Again, the devil took [Jesus] to a very high mountain and showed him all the kingdoms of the world and their splendor; and he said to him, "All these I will give you, if you will fall down and worship me." Jesus said to him, "Away with you, Satan! for it is written, 'Worship the Lord your God, and serve only him.'" Then the devil left him, and suddenly angels came and waited on him.

To ponder

By your helpless infant years,
by your life of want and tears,
by your days of deep distress
in the savage wilderness,
by the dread, mysterious hour

14

of the insulting tempter's pow'r,
turn, oh, turn a fav'ring eye;
hear our penitential cry!
—Robert Grant, "Savior, when in dust to you," ELW 601, st. 2

Worthy of worship

The first two temptations of Jesus began with the devil saying, "If you are the Son of God. . . ." But by the third temptation it seems that patience is wearing thin. The insulting tempter skips the formalities: "Fall down and worship me."

Even if we rule "all the kingdoms of the world and their splendor," we are nothing as human beings if we abandon our Creator. We are sons and daughters of the Holy One. This identity is both important to remember and easy to forget. When the savage, scorching desert encroaches upon us, we can feel so isolated. It's tempting to turn to anyone or anything to find relief.

Martin Luther reminds us to turn to our baptism. Every day. Begin the day by giving thanks for the little resurrection that this day is. And remember that in baptismal grace it is God to whom we offer our worship. This doesn't necessarily mean that temptations will go away. But it does mean that, despite the devil's craftiest tactics, we will stand in the power of the risen Christ.

Prayer

God, you alone are worthy of our worship and our praise. Save us from the desert of loneliness and despair and remind us always of your presence and your love. Amen.

Matthew 4:23-25

Jesus went throughout Galilee, teaching in their synagogues and proclaiming the good news of the kingdom and curing every disease and every sickness among the people. So his fame spread throughout all Syria, and they brought to him all the sick, those who were afflicted with various diseases and pains, demoniacs, epileptics, and paralytics, and he cured them. And great crowds followed him from Galilee, the Decapolis, Jerusalem, Judea, and from beyond the Jordan.

To ponder

We think in generalities, but we live in detail. —Alfred North Whitehead, *Modes of Thought*

Right down to the smallest detail

These three verses from Matthew's gospel are packed with detail about the beginning of Jesus' ministry. The various sorts of diseases Jesus heals are cataloged. The places he goes are likewise recounted in specific detail. Teaching, proclaiming, and curing take on flesh and bones in the real lives of real people from the real places Jesus visits.

There is nothing theoretical about the life of Jesus among us. We may think of him in generalities—love, compassion, mercy—but his life intersected with real people and had a profound effect on them. Whether it was in Galilee, the Decapolis, Jerusalem, Judea, or far beyond the Jordan, Jesus healed real people dealing with real difficulties.

Jesus does not see us as just one more face in the crowd. He sees us and claims us for the unique and beloved children of God we were created to be. He knows our inmost thoughts and is present in the mountaintop experiences of our lives as well as the Monday monotony. He will find us wherever we are and come in close to the specific diseases and pains of our lives. We may think in generalities, as Alfred North Whitehead notes, but we live in detail. And that's where Jesus finds us.

Prayer

Jesus, we thank you for always being near. We are blessed by the wondrous love of your intimate embrace of our lives. Welcome to the details. Amen.

March 4

Matthew 8:29, 32, 34

Suddenly [two demoniacs] shouted, "What have you to do with us, Son of God? Have you come here to torment us before the time?" . . . And [Jesus] said to [the demons], "Go!" So they came out and entered the swine. . . . Then the whole town came out to meet Jesus; and when they saw him, they begged him to leave their neighborhood.

To ponder

I am still haunted by a long conversation I had with a man who was a member of one of my early congregations. . . . He had a stunning vision of the presence of the risen Christ . . . [and] had never told anyone about it before. . . . He explained, "The reason why I told no one was I was too afraid that it was true. And if it's true that Jesus was really real, that he had come personally to me, what then? I'd have to change my whole life." —William H. Willimon, *Undone by Easter*

Claimed

Jesus Christ, exorcist, has come to destroy your demons. Maybe this sounds alien to you, but make no mistake. We are possessed. What possesses you? Is it drugs or alcohol? Money? Envy? Shame and guilt? Fear?

Only Jesus can drive out our demons. Our clergy aren't trained to drive out demons; exorcisms have been exorcised from most of our practices. Well, except in our baptismal liturgy. Did you realize this includes a rite of "exorcism"? Together we renounce "the devil and all the forces that defy God," "the powers of this world that rebel against God," and "the ways of sin that draw [us] from God" (ELW, p. 229). Demons, get out!

Like the townspeople in Matthew's story, sometimes we too would rather have Jesus leave us alone with our demons, the devils we know. But when Jesus drives out our demons, we're set free—free to follow him. God only knows where that will take us.

Prayer

Holy God, you have set us free. Give us courage to follow you out of our comfort zones and into the world you love. Amen.

March 5

Matthew 9:2, 5-8

Some people were carrying a paralyzed man lying on a bed....
[Jesus said,] "Which is easier, to say, 'Your sins are forgiven,' or to
say, 'Stand up and walk'? But so that you may know that the Son
of Man has authority on earth to forgive sins"—he then said to
the paralytic—"Stand up, take your bed and go to your home."
And he stood up and went to his home. When the crowds saw it,
they were filled with awe, and they glorified God.

To ponder

Space is very beautiful. The dark velvet of the sky, the blue halo of
the Earth, and the lakes and rivers and fields and cloud formations
speeding by. All around there is perfect silence.... The panorama
is calm, majestic. —Valentin Lebedev, in *The Overview Effect*

Awestruck

I saw it for the first time when I was nine or ten years old, on an overnight hike with the Girl Scouts. We unfurled our bedrolls and sleeping bags in an open field, and as I lay on my back and looked up, there it was—the Milky Way, resplendent above me. Billions of stars, flung across the sky, so many that they were clustered in a shimmering haze of light. I lay awake for a long time, awestruck.

Think about a time when you were filled with awe. Soviet cosmonaut Valentin Lebedev experienced this when he saw the Earth in space, a tiny part of a vast universe. Maybe you've heard the pulsing heart of a developing fetus, or the sound of your own blood rushing through your arteries and veins, or maybe you've seen a living brain lighting up as electricity leaps over the synapses. Maybe you have witnessed the birth of a child or kept vigil with someone who was dying.

In moments like these, how do we respond? The witnesses to the exorcism in Matthew 8 reacted fearfully and told Jesus to get out of town. But when the crowds in today's story see a man with paralysis get up and walk, they are awestruck. Glory to God!

Prayer

Holy God, heaven and earth are filled with your glory. Draw us to you in love and wonder. Amen.

March 6

Matthew 9:9-11

[Jesus] saw a man called Matthew sitting at the tax booth; and he said to him, "Follow me." And he got up and followed him. And as he sat at dinner in the house, many tax collectors and sinners came and were sitting with him and his disciples. When the Pharisees saw this, they said to his disciples, "Why does your teacher eat with tax collectors and sinners?"

To ponder

We didn't have a lot of rules [at the food pantry at St. Gregory, an Episcopal congregation in San Francisco]. You could be a drunk or junkie, but you couldn't volunteer if you were high. You couldn't steal food, call people names, or get in fights.

Otherwise anyone was welcome to jump in and start working. We were making a bet that what Jesus suggested was true: when you begin to expand your ideas of who the right people are, when you break down boundaries to share food with strangers, God shows up. —Sara Miles, *Jesus Freak*

The company he keeps

The Pharisees are scandalized by the company Jesus keeps. After calling Matthew from his tax table and then, it seems, going to Matthew's house for dinner, Jesus sits with the other guests—tax collectors and other assorted "sinners."

We're tempted to see the Pharisees as narrow-minded critics. Surely we are not like them! But at the time, the Pharisees weren't alone in their dislike of tax collectors. Tax collectors were hated agents of the Roman government who collected money for the empire. They often enriched themselves in the process by extorting more than was owed.

The Pharisees don't want to share table fellowship with tax collectors and "sinners," and they are offended when Jesus does. Who is it that we wouldn't want at the table with us? Unlike us, Jesus isn't concerned about the company he keeps. He sees all people as sinners in need of wholeness and healing.

Prayer

Holy God, thank you for showing up at the table where you are both guest and host. Help us to see others as you see them—your beloved ones. Amen.

Matthew 12:1-2, 6-8

Jesus went through the grainfields on the sabbath; his disciples were hungry, and they began to pluck heads of grain and to eat. When the Pharisees saw it, they said to him, "Look, your disciples are doing what is not lawful to do on the sabbath." . . . [Jesus said,] "I tell, something greater than the temple is here. But if you had known what this means, 'I desire mercy and not sacrifice,' you would not have condemned the guiltless. For the Son of Man is lord of the sabbath."

To ponder

As long as we continue to live as if we are what we do, what we have, and what other people think about us, we will be filled with judgments, opinions, evaluations, and condemnations. We will remain addicted to the need to put people and things in their "right" place. To the degree that we can embrace the truth that our identity is not rooted in our success, power, or popularity, but in God's infinite love, to that degree can we let go of our need to judge. —Henri Nouwen, *Here and Now*

Your inner Pharisee

In the gospels the Pharisees are often adversaries of Jesus, challenging his teaching and threatened by his huge following. But it's important to recognize that they are also faithful leaders who care about their community, who know and teach the laws and structures that govern daily life. They are insiders with the strengths—and blind spots—of insiders.

Does that sound like anyone you know?

Those of us who are faithful churchgoers, active members of congregations, or church leaders often lament when others don't follow the rules. Why can't people give more, volunteer more, take a more active role in the church? After all, we're welcoming!—why don't more people come here to worship with us on Sunday?

When we let go of judgment, we are all set free to become the people we're meant to be, and to see Jesus at work in the whole world.

Prayer

Lord of the sabbath, help us to remember that you're the judge—we don't have to set the whole world straight. And thank you for your mercy and wondrous love that will not let us go. Amen.

March 8 / Lent 2

Matthew 14:1-2, 5

Herod the ruler heard reports about Jesus; and he said to his servants, "This is John the Baptist; he has been raised from the dead, and for this reason these powers are at work in him." . . . Though Herod wanted to put [Jesus] to death, he feared the crowd, because they regarded him as a prophet.

To ponder

Herod symbolizes the terrible destruction that fearful people can leave in their wake if their fear is unacknowledged, if they have power but can only use it in furtive, pathetic, and futile attempts at self-preservation.

Herod's fear is like a mighty wind; it cannot be seen, but its effects dominate the landscape. —Kathleen Norris, *Amazing Grace*

Fear

Fear is a "mighty wind" indeed. The wreckage left by the toxic wind of fear is evident everywhere. We are afraid of the unknown, afraid of one another, afraid of poor health, afraid of death, and afraid of what the future holds for our loved ones, congregations, and communities. Fearing that we won't have enough, we hold tight to what we have and are reluctant to share. Fearing the claims of those who have been excluded or marginalized, we react with resentment, anger, and even violence.

Tyrants themselves experience fear, knowing that force cannot compel obedience forever. So it is with Herod the king. He imprisons John the Baptist and has him beheaded, but then fears that John has come back from the dead. Herod fears Jesus and his message of God's kingdom too, but fear of the crowd prevents him from doing away with Jesus—for the time being, anyway.

Although the threat to Jesus' life increases as we continue through Matthew's gospel, Jesus keeps moving toward Jerusalem and the cross. He refuses to give in to fear or to answer violence with violence. On the cross we see the power of vulnerable love. In the resurrection, we witness wondrous love stronger than all our fears—even stronger than death.

Prayer

Holy God, our fears keep us from loving and serving you and others. Drive out our fears with your perfect love. Amen.

March 9

Matthew 14:15-17, 19

The disciples came to [Jesus] and said, "This is a deserted place, and the hour is now late; send the crowds away so that they may go into the villages and buy food for themselves." Jesus said to them, "They need not go away; you give them something to eat." They replied, "We have nothing here but five loaves and two fish." . . . Taking the five loaves and the two fish, [Jesus] looked up to heaven, and blessed and broke the loaves.

To ponder

Take what you have—whatever you have—take it into your hands and hold it lightly, very lightly. Then *bless* it—thank God for what you have and make it holy by giving it away for love. Then *break* it—sorry, but you have to tear it up to share it, there is no way to keep it all in one nice piece. And finally, give it—to whoever is standing in front of you, beside you—spread it around, and never mind that there does not seem to be enough for everyone. —Barbara Brown Taylor, *Mixed Blessings*

Not enough?

In our society we sometimes feel as though there's not enough to go around. Not enough work for our young people. Not enough money. Not enough people, or resources, or willing volunteers in our congregations.

Jesus' disciples look at the huge crowd and give him the news. "Nothing here but five loaves and two fishes." Not enough. Jesus blesses what they have, however, and not only is the hungry crowd of five thousand fed, but there are twelve baskets of leftovers!

Jesus can take whatever we have, bless it, and make it more than enough. Bring what you have to him and see it multiply. With a gift to world hunger, for example, a little bit of money becomes animals for food, wells for clean water, schools for children. What might Jesus do with an open heart, or with a congregation committed to growing in faith and love?

Prayer

God of abundance, feed us, fill us, and send us to share what you have blessed. Amen.

March 10

Matthew 16:13-16

Now when Jesus came into the district of Caesarea Philippi, he asked his disciples, "Who do people say that the Son of Man is?" And they said, "Some say John the Baptist, but others Elijah, and still others Jeremiah or one of the prophets." He said to them, "But who do you say that I am?" Simon Peter answered, "You are the Messiah, the Son of the living God."

To ponder

The mother may give her child to suck her milk, but our precious mother Jesus, he may feed us with himself, and does so most courteously and most tenderly with the blessed sacrament that is the precious food of true life. —Julian of Norwich, in *An Explorer's Guide to Julian of Norwich*

Naming Jesus

Julian of Norwich, a fourteenth-century mystic, called him "Christ our mother." Jesus compared himself to a mother hen, gathering her chicks under her wings (Matthew 23:37; Luke 13:34). Others called him Mighty Counselor. Prince of Peace. King. A glutton and a drunkard. Teacher. Rabbi. Friend. Prophet. Redeemer. Holy One. Lamb of God. Messiah. Son of David, son of Joseph, Son of God. Lord and Savior.

He called himself the good shepherd. The gate. The bread of life. The light of the world. The true vine. Lord of the sabbath. The Son of Man. The way, and the truth, and the life.

How do these many images of Jesus challenge, bless, change, or comfort you? What name do you call out in prayer?

Prayer

Holy One, you have called our names in baptism. Hear us as we call your name in times of trouble, celebration, gratitude, grief, and joy. Amen.

Matthew 16:21-23

From that time on, Jesus began to show his disciples that he must go to Jerusalem and undergo great suffering at the hands of the elders and chief priests and scribes, and be killed, and on the third day be raised. And Peter took him aside and began to rebuke him, saying, "God forbid it, Lord! This must never happen to you." But he turned and said to Peter, "Get behind me, Satan! You are a stumbling block to me; for you are setting your mind not on divine things but on human things."

To ponder

"But how am I to know the good side from the bad?" he asked, puzzled. "You will know," Yoda answered. "When you are at peace . . . calm, passive." —Donald F. Glut, *Star Wars: The Empire Strikes Back*

Voices

We have so many voices in our hearts and minds on a regular basis, sometimes simultaneously. It can be challenging to decipher where they are coming from. How can we tell if God is speaking to us? Or when it's just our own minds at work? How can we tell if there's some other influence at work in us?

Perhaps in an effort to be protective, Peter inadvertently allows himself to be a mouthpiece for Satan—and a stumbling block for Jesus. This scene between two friends is an uncomfortable one to read. Peter and Jesus both struggle with different voices and messages all around them and within them.

I wish it were as simple to know good from bad, what is best to do and what is not, as Yoda makes it sound. Sometimes it is, but not always. What Yoda gets at, though, is to trust your instincts. (This may sound like I'm advising you to ignore God. On the contrary, your instincts were given to you by God to use.)

Prayer

Speaking God, help us to trust your voice within us and around us. Amen.

March 12

Matthew 16:24-26

Then Jesus told his disciples, "If any want to become my followers, let them deny themselves and take up their cross and follow me. For those who want to save their life will lose it, and those who lose their life for my sake will find it. For what will it profit them if they gain the whole world but forfeit their life? Or what will they give in return for their life?"

To ponder

Behold the life-giving cross, on which was hung the Savior of the whole world. —Good Friday procession of the cross

Crosses

Out of wondrous love and sacrifice, Jesus takes up his cross and dies. Now we call that cross "life-giving" in Good Friday worship.

Crosses come in all shapes and sizes. Anytime we sacrifice or deny ourselves for the sake of someone else, we carry a cross. Here's what this might look like in everyday life: the nurse who puts on her scrubs to heal others, the police officer who puts on her bullet-proof vest to protect others, the pastor who puts on her stole to guide others, the artist who uses her paintbrush to inspire others, or the parent who puts on her peanut-butter-and-jelly-stained shirt to care for her family. All these callings involve a strong element of sacrifice to be successful, and they have their own symbols, like Jesus' cross. What symbolizes the cross you bear?

Child of God, the Almighty knows that your cross can be heavy. Know that you do not endure it alone, and that through the cross of Jesus you have abundant life.

Prayer

Sacrificing God, strengthen us as we take up our crosses with you. Amen.

Matthew 17:1-4

Jesus took with him Peter and James and his brother John and led them up a high mountain, by themselves. And he was transfigured before them, and his face shone like the sun, and his clothes became dazzling white. Suddenly there appeared to them Moses and Elijah, talking with him. Then Peter said to Jesus, "Lord, it is good for us to be here; if you wish, I will make three dwellings here, one for you, one for Moses, and one for Elijah."

To ponder

[Zach] had gone from seeing beauty in the midst of suffering to creating it. He had taken this thing that could have suffocated him with despair and stripped it down until all that was left was hope.
—Laura Sobiech, *Fly a Little Higher*

Hope

Jesus had been talking a lot about death—predicting his own death and saying that his followers would have to take up their own crosses. Imagine how this sounded to his closest followers, the disciples. They had given up so much for him already. They might have been thinking, "Was this all for nothing? Should we cut our losses now?"

Then, with perfect timing, God provides Peter, James, and John with a mind-blowing mountaintop experience. Surely any doubts they had as to the nature of this rabbi and teacher are gone now. Well, maybe not—they were human, after all. But for a moment, they receive a glimpse into something bigger than they can possibly imagine. Now they know that God is up to something beyond their comprehension. And that, dear child of God, is the makings of hope.

As followers on this side of the cross, we know things are going to get worse for Jesus and the disciples before they get better. Peter, James, and John will need to hold this mountaintop experience in their hearts to get through what lies ahead.

Prayer

God of hope, remind us of the hope-filled moments you have created for us, especially during troubling times ahead. Amen.

March 14

Matthew 17:5-7

While [Peter] was still speaking, suddenly a bright cloud overshadowed them, and from the cloud a voice said, "This is my Son, the Beloved; with him I am well pleased; listen to him!" When the disciples heard this, they fell to the ground and were overcome by fear. But Jesus came and touched them, saying, "Get up and do not be afraid."

To ponder

Mothers and infants do an enormous amount of touching. The first emotional comfort, touching and being touched by our mother, remains the ultimate memory of selfless love, which stays with us life long. —Diane Ackerman, *A Natural History of the Senses*

Touch

Our dog Pearl likes to take baths. Her breed doesn't take to water naturally, so at first we were stumped as to why she'd jump in the tub without even being asked. Then one day it dawned on me. When we first got Pearl as a puppy, she was living outside on a goat farm in the sweltering heat. She was dirty and her fur was matted with prickly burrs. As Pearl rode in the back seat of the car on the way to her new home, my daughter picked out all those burrs. When we arrived home we immediately took our new puppy to the bathtub. That back seat and that tub were the places where Pearl first received our touch and our love. So of course she loves to take baths—and car rides.

Touch can be so powerful. When the disciples fall down in fear on the mountaintop, the first thing Jesus does is touch them. Before he speaks to them, before he reasons with them, he comforts them with a touch.

One of the things I love about worship during Lent is how tactile it is: rough ashes on our foreheads, refreshing water on our feet—not to mention all the handshakes and hugs.

Child of God, may you always remember the power of touch, and use it wisely and lovingly.

Prayer

Loving God, we ask for your healing presence on those who have been harmed by touch, especially in the church. Help us bring a touch of your love into the world. Amen.

March 15 / Lent 3

Matthew 17:9-10, 12

As they were coming down the mountain, Jesus ordered [Peter, James, and John], "Tell no one about the vision until after the Son of Man has been raised from the dead." And the disciples asked him, "Why, then, do the scribes say that Elijah must come first?" He replied, ". . . Elijah has already come, and they did not recognize him, but they did to him whatever they pleased. So also the Son of Man is about to suffer at their hands."

To ponder

Even in church, a place where many people seek solace in times of grief and sorrow, families of prisoners often keep secret the imprisonment of their children or relatives. As one woman responded when asked if she could turn to church members for support, "Church? I wouldn't dare tell anyone at church." Far from being a place of comfort or refuge, churches can be a place where judgment, shame, and contempt are felt most acutely. —Michelle Alexander, *The New Jim Crow*

Secrets

Jesus asks Peter, James, and John to wait to tell others about what they have seen on the mountaintop. Would the disciples better understand—and share—their experience after Jesus died and was raised? Did they have trouble keeping this secret, the way we have trouble keeping a surprise party a surprise?

It's healthy—and even fun—to have people in your life with whom you can share secrets. Think of the way children light up when someone lets them in on a secret, like the hiding place for the Christmas gifts or the birthday cake Grandma isn't expecting.

But as we are painfully aware, some secrets are unhealthy. Michelle Alexander writes that families who have a relative in prison often keep this a secret. These families find that sharing their secret in church doesn't result in care and support, so they tell no one.

Child of God, whatever your secrets, they are always safe with God.

Prayer

God of safety and security, may we create times and spaces for people to freely share their lives—even their secrets. Amen.

Matthew 21:7-9

[The disciples] brought the donkey and the colt, and put their cloaks on them, and [Jesus] sat on them. A very large crowd spread their cloaks on the road, and others cut branches from the trees and spread them on the road. The crowds that went ahead of him and that followed were shouting, "Hosanna to the Son of David! Blessed is the one who comes in the name of the Lord!"

To ponder

What would it look like to create a church insistent that the world is in desperate need of a more just and generous expression of the Christian faith? Where the love and grace of God is allowed to freely flow and freely be received? Where the radical concept of inclusion and welcoming everybody suddenly is revealed to not be radical at all, but actually [lies] at the foundation of the gospel? A church where over and over again we insist that you are a loved child of God, fully welcome in the family? —Colby Martin, *Unclobber*

Welcome

The Jerusalem crowds greet Jesus with the biggest welcome they can muster. By the time he enters Jerusalem, "the whole city [is] in turmoil, asking, 'Who is this?'" (Matthew 21:10). By the end of the week, however, shouts of "Hosanna!" turn to "Crucify him!" How does this happen?

To be fair, we aren't that different from the crowds that usher Jesus into Jerusalem. We welcome Jesus into our cities, our sanctuaries, our homes, our hearts—as long as he makes us feel comfortable. We're not as quick to welcome the Jesus who urges us to change our hearts and lives.

I think we do the same with other people. When we say all are welcome, do we really mean to include *everyone*? Do we welcome people only as long as we feel comfortable around them?

Child of God, Jesus welcomes all people and all of what makes you who you are.

Prayer

Welcoming God, give us hearts and lives that welcome you and welcome all to be fully part of your realm. Amen.

March 17

Matthew 26:3-5, 14-16

Then the chief priests and the elders of the people gathered in the palace of the high priest, who was called Caiaphas, and they conspired to arrest Jesus by stealth and kill him. But they said, "Not during the festival, or there may be a riot among the people." . . . Then [Judas Iscariot] went to the chief priests and said, "What will you give me if I betray him to you?" They paid him thirty pieces of silver. And from that moment he began to look for an opportunity to betray him.

To ponder

The meaning of Christmas is to give of yourself—to open up the joy in your heart and share it generously. If you do this properly,

then every day will feel like . . . well, like Christmas. —Bradley
Trevor Greive, *Every Day Is Christmas*

Holiday

The religious elite come up with a scheme to do away with Jesus.
The plot is about to unfold, but wait—not now, not during the
festival. For a time the holiday keeps the conspirators at bay and
stays their murderous hands. Imagine if they had lived instead as
if every day were a festival day.

Have you ever said or done things differently because of a special occasion? Maybe your child misbehaved and you let it slide
because . . . well, it was her birthday. Or maybe you made an extra
effort to be kind and gracious to your spouse on your anniversary.
Or on Thanksgiving Day you wrote down some things that fill
you with gratitude.

Imagine if we treated every day as a holiday or a special occasion—thinking things through before reacting or complaining,
giving people the benefit of the doubt, treating others as God's
beloved children. Can you imagine a world like that?

Prayer

God of celebration, fill us with your joy so that it spills out on
everyone around us every day. Amen.

Matthew 26:20-22, 25

When it was evening, [Jesus] took his place with the twelve; and while they were eating, he said, "Truly I tell you, one of you will betray me." And they became greatly distressed and began to say to him one after another, "Surely not I, Lord?" . . . Judas, who betrayed him, said, "Surely not I, Rabbi?"

To ponder

All the persons of faith I know are sinners, doubters, uneven performers. We are secure not because we are sure of ourselves but because we trust that God is sure of us. —Eugene H. Peterson, *A Long Obedience in the Same Direction*

Security

"Surely not I," the disciples said, one by one, all around the room. Judas, who must have been crawling out of his skin from guilt, fear, or conflicted conviction, said it too: "Surely not I."

Jesus responded matter-of-factly: *Yes, one of you will betray me.* Maybe he wasn't unnerved by the situation because he had sat around the table with sinners plenty of times before. In fact, Jesus never sat around a table on earth that wasn't filled with sinners. Likewise, you and I never sit at a table that isn't occupied with sinners. (That goes for dining alone too.)

Jesus is not surprised to discover that his followers are doubters, betrayers—sinners. We are the ones who are surprised, valiantly claiming, "Surely not I." But our security rests not in ourselves, but in the fact that Jesus loves sinners.

Prayer

Show us the freedom, O Lord, in naming ourselves as sinners and admitting we are not sure of ourselves. Show us the security, Lord, in knowing you are sure in your love for us. Amen.

Matthew 26:26-28

While they were eating, Jesus took a loaf of bread, and after blessing it he broke it, gave it to the disciples, and said, "Take, eat; this is my body." Then he took a cup, and after giving thanks he gave it to them, saying, "Drink from it, all of you; for this is my blood of the covenant, which is poured out for many for the forgiveness of sins."

To ponder

If the needs that ought to move and induce us to confession were clearly indicated, there would be no need for coercion or force. Their own consciences would persuade Christians. . . . They would rejoice and act like poor, miserable beggars who hear that a rich gift of money or clothes is being given out at a certain place; they

would . . . run there as fast as they could so as not to miss the gift.
—Martin Luther, "The Large Catechism"

Take

When we teach table manners to children we say, "Don't take food without asking," "Don't take more than your share," and "Don't take the last piece without offering it to someone else first." And when we teach young ones about holy communion we talk about receiving, not taking. We show children how to layer their hands one on top of the other, slightly cupping them, ready to receive.

Jesus commands us, however, to take the bread and cup. Take and eat. Do not be passive receivers. Take! *Take what I am offering you.* Drink. Drink from the cup. Be bold. Be sure. Be desperate even. Do not hold back from these gifts. Don't wait. Take the very presence of God offered to you, given in a way that you can hold in your hands, forgiveness you can taste. As Luther would say, run after the gift as fast as you can. Take, eat!

Prayer

Fill us with a hunger, Lord, for your gift of redemption. Fill us with such hunger that we lose all hesitation, maybe even our manners, to take what you offer—forgiveness and love. Amen.

Matthew 26:31-34

Jesus said to [the disciples], "You will all become deserters because of me this night. . . . But after I am raised up, I will go ahead of you to Galilee." Peter said to him, "Though all become deserters because of you, I will never desert you." Jesus said to him, "Truly I tell you, this very night, before the cock crows, you will deny me three times."

To ponder

Prone to wander, Lord, I feel it;
prone to leave the God I love.
Here's my heart, oh, take and seal it;
seal it for thy courts above.
—Robert Robinson, "Come, thou Fount of every blessing,"
    ELW 807, st. 3

I will never desert you

In some form or another we are all "prone to wander" from faith, from the church, from God. Maybe we walk away from the church after experiencing hurt in a place that is supposed to heal. Maybe the understanding of faith and the Bible we received as children doesn't hold up to the questions and complexities we encounter as adults. Maybe at some point life hands us sorrow and disappointment so deep we turn away not only from church, but from God. Or we might slowly wander off over the course of many weeks or months as life pulls us in other directions, until one day we realize we can't remember how long it's been since we participated in worship or prayed.

Jesus is familiar with all the ways we wander off. And even as he predicts that the disciples will desert him, he says, "After I am raised up, I will go ahead of you to Galilee." Wow, what an amazing promise to the disciples—and to us! When we walk away or wander off from faith, Jesus goes ahead of us and waits to beckon us home. We may desert him, but Jesus will never desert us.

Prayer

Good Shepherd, you are well practiced at finding those who wander off. When we walk away and leave faith behind, show us that we are not alone. You go ahead of us and will lead us home. Amen.

Matthew 26:36, 39-40

Then Jesus went with them to a place called Gethsemane; and
he said to his disciples, "Sit here while I go over there and pray."
. . . And going a little farther, he threw himself on the ground
and prayed, "My Father, if it is possible, let this cup pass from me;
yet not what I want but what you want." Then he came to the
disciples and found them sleeping; and he said to Peter, "So, could
you not stay awake with me one hour?"

To ponder

Faith, thankfully, does not preclude doubt. It consists of staking
your life on the rumor of grace. —Michael Gerson, "I was hospitalized for depression: Faith helped me remember how to live"

Struggle

In the garden of Gethsemane Jesus doesn't have it all together. He slumps down to the ground. Does he do this out of sheer exhaustion? Does he throw himself down the way a child does, embodying resistance? Regardless of the circumstances, this image of Jesus confronts us: he is the Son of God *and* fully human. It is difficult for us to take this in. And yet we could not relate to one who sails through every aspect of human life never experiencing temptation, hurt, or pain. But a Messiah who can relate to doubt and despair? Well, tell us about this one.

At some point in our lives all of us experience some degree of doubt, despair, or depression. In these times, we might throw ourselves on the ground. Slump in exhaustion. Doubt the purpose before us. Resist with the full weight of our bodies. Throw our hands up in despair when we can't count on our friends to be there for us.

This scene from the garden of Gethsemane, however, offers us a sign of hope. When Jesus threw himself to the ground, he called out to God in prayer. Even in the most desperate of times, we can call out to God, knowing God is there for us too.

Prayer

When doubt and despair level us, O God, turn us to you in prayer, and whisper words of grace in our ears. Amen.

March 22 / Lent 4

Matthew 26:42-46

Again [Jesus] went away for the second time and prayed, "My Father, if this cannot pass unless I drink it, your will be done." Again he came and found [the disciples] sleeping, for their eyes were heavy. So leaving them again, he went away and prayed for the third time, saying the same words. Then he came to the disciples and said to them, "Are you still sleeping and taking your rest? . . . Get up, let us be going. See, my betrayer is at hand."

To ponder

When I was sinking down, sinking down, sinking down,
when I was sinking down, sinking down,
when I was sinking down beneath God's righteous frown,
Christ laid aside his crown for my soul, for my soul,

Christ laid aside his crown for my soul.
—"What wondrous love is this," ELW 666, st. 2

Asleep on the watch

As a person who struggles to stay awake after ten p.m., I read Matthew's account of the night in Gethsemane with sympathy for the heavy-eyed disciples. But deep down, this scene isn't so much about sleep as it is about a friend in agony. Jesus in the garden is not filled with divine calm, but with human distress. The disciples who recently declared, "Surely not I" and "I will never desert you" are now asleep. In a mild, sleepy way they have begun to desert Jesus already.

From the outside it is frustrating to watch the disciples fall short again and again. Maybe it is even more frustrating because they remind us of ourselves. The disciples will not be the heroes of this story. They won't somehow get it together and save the day. The saving can only be done by Jesus, who comes to accept God's will during this struggle in the garden. When Jesus returns to find the disciples still sleeping, he says (with a sigh?), *Get up, let's go. The path I need to take is clear.*

Prayer

Lord, when we are weary and when we are wearying, when we are sinking down, remind us of your wondrous love for us. Amen.

Matthew 26:47-50, 56

Judas, one of the twelve, arrived; with him was a large crowd with swords and clubs, from the chief priests and the elders of the people. Now the betrayer had given them a sign, saying, "The one I will kiss is the man; arrest him." At once he came up to Jesus and said, "Greetings, Rabbi!" and kissed him. Jesus said to him, "Friend, do what you are here to do." Then they came and laid hands on Jesus and arrested him. . . . Then all the disciples deserted him and fled.

To ponder

[In worship] after reading from the memoirs of the apostles, and from the Old Testament prophets, the president . . . preached a sermon, at the end of which everyone stood for a solemn prayer ending in the kiss of peace. —Henry Chadwick, *The Early Church*

Kiss of peace

In the early church the sharing of the peace in worship involved not a handshake but a kiss of peace. The kiss Jesus receives from Judas appears to be that greeting's opposite—a kiss of betrayal, with a background of clubs and swords. And yet it is also a kiss of peace.

This night in the garden of Gethsemane has been a night of disappointment, frustration, and despair. The failings of Jesus' friends have been made clear. Despite their exclamations of "Surely not I" and their adamant words about not betraying or deserting him, Jesus knows that the disciples will fall asleep again. They will scatter with the wind and desert him. They cannot save themselves. Jesus is the only one who can save them—and us. And so Jesus peacefully accepts Judas's greeting and kiss, saying, "Friend, do what you are here to do."

Jesus, too, will do what he is here to do.

Prayer

Prince of Peace, we fall short, and still, you call us friends. You save us because we cannot save ourselves. Help us to share this news with others, and to bring your peace to the world. Amen.

March 24

Matthew 26:57-58

Those who had arrested Jesus took him to Caiaphas the high
priest, in whose house the scribes and the elders had gathered.
But Peter was following him at a distance, as far as the courtyard
of the high priest; and going inside, he sat with the guards in
order to see how this would end.

To ponder

We live in a brutal world. But in the life of Christ and the work
of the Holy Spirit we glimpse redemption and participate in it....
Our work, our times in prayer and service, our small days lived
graciously, missionally, and faithfully will bear fruit that we can't
yet see. —Tish Harrison Warren, *The Liturgy of the Ordinary*

God sees all

Peter gets as close as he can to the religious trial of Jesus to watch and wait, to see how this drama will unfold before his eyes and beyond his control. From a short distance away, what does Peter see? Does he see the fulfillment of the long-awaited Messiah? Does he see a friend and teacher wrongly accused and powerless to fight back? Does he watch for his own sake or for the sake of the whole world? And as he watches, is Peter full of despair or hope or both?

In some way, we are all watching and waiting to see what will happen next in the gospel, and in life. We see through the lenses of our hopes and dreams, our expectations and longings. All too often in the face of suffering, the pain and heartbreak overwhelm our field of vision. And yet, we hold onto the baptismal promise that God is present in all suffering and heartbreak. When our vision is clouded by fear and pain, God sees all. God holds the despair and the hope, drawing us into the vision of life and grace in Christ. We weep and dare to look on, waiting for what comes next.

Prayer

Merciful God, open our eyes to see your salvation in Jesus Christ for the sake of the whole world. In times of suffering and pain, help us to see mercy and hope. Reveal your love and signs of new life in all circumstances. Amen.

Matthew 26:59-63

Now the chief priests and the whole council were looking for false testimony against Jesus so that they might put him to death, but they found none, though many false witnesses came forward. At last two came forward and said, "This fellow said, 'I am able to destroy the temple of God and to build it in three days.'" The high priest stood up and said, "Have you no answer? What is it that they testify against you?" But Jesus was silent.

To ponder

Holy silence is spacious and inviting. You can drink it down. . . . During congregational silences, in meditation rooms or halls, in prison cells and meeting rooms, in silent confession at church, all these screwed-up people like us, with tangled lives and minds, find their hearts opening through quiet focus. —Anne Lamott, *Hallelujah Anyway*

Silent impact

Amid all the noise of the crowds, the council, and the witnesses, Jesus is silent. This silence is not an absence of sound or a stubborn refusal to respond to an inquisitor. Rather, Jesus' silence is full of presence. Jesus' silence witnesses to God's power and presence in the depths of salvation.

In our lives today, silence is often awkward or difficult to find. Music plays in the background. Vehicles rumble by our homes. Household appliances and machines add subtle noise to our lives. Encountering silence usually makes us uncomfortable until we can find a way to fill in the seemingly absent space. Silent pauses in worship make us wonder what is missing or what comes next. A question met with silence is cause for worry and conflict.

But Jesus' silence ripples with peace. No words are necessary to proclaim God's power and presence. Christ's silence invites us to contemplate God's presence in the gospel account and in our lives and faith communities. We are invited into this full silence, not as individuals, but as the very body of Christ today.

Prayer

God of the silence, draw us into the unending harmony of your presence beyond words and noise. Keep us still for a moment, that we might yearn for and notice our hearts opening in hope. Amen.

March 26

Matthew 26:63b-66

The high priest said to [Jesus], "I put you under oath before the living God, tell us if you are the Messiah, the Son of God." Jesus said to him, "You have said so. But I tell you,

> From now on you will see the Son of Man
> seated at the right hand of Power
> and coming on the clouds of heaven."

Then the high priest tore his clothes and said, "He has blasphemed! . . . What is your verdict?" They answered, "He deserves death."

To ponder

I hope no one who reads this book has been quite as miserable as Susan and Lucy were that night; but if you have been—if you've been up all night and cried till you have no more tears left in you—you will know that there comes in the end a sort of quietness. . . . But at last Lucy noticed two other things. One was that the sky on the East side of the hill was a little less dark than it had been an hour ago. The other was some movement going on in the grass at her feet. —C. S. Lewis, *The Lion, the Witch, and the Wardrobe*

The storm

The storm of Jesus' passion is in full swing as he responds to the high priest by describing who he is: the Son of Man, the Messiah. In response to this, the high priest reveals his inability to see this truth by tearing his clothes and accusing Jesus of blasphemy.

At the height of this storm, the contrasts come to light. Humanity's sinfulness cannot fully see the grace of God in this moment, even as Christ's divinity becomes more and more clear. When the storm has fully passed, the resurrection will make plain the gift of salvation through Christ. The sun comes out again, and we see with a new acuity and clarity. As in baptism, the dust of our lives is washed away, and life is made new again.

Prayer

God of power and might, help us endure the storms of life. Give us faith and courage to watch and wait for the clouds to pass. Inspire us with the hope of new beginnings. Amen.

Matthew 26:69-75

A servant-girl came to [Peter] and said, "You also were with Jesus the Galilean." But he denied it before all of them, saying, "I do not know what you are talking about." . . . Another servant-girl saw him, and she said to the bystanders, "This man was with Jesus of Nazareth." Again he denied it with an oath, "I do not know the man." After a little while the bystanders came up and said to Peter, "Certainly you are also one of them, for your accent betrays you." Then he began to curse, and he swore an oath, "I do not know the man!" At that moment the cock crowed. . . . And he went out and wept bitterly.

To ponder

Practicing authenticity can feel like a daunting choice—there's risk involved in putting your true self out in the world. But I believe there's even more risk in hiding yourself and your gifts from the world. —Brené Brown, *The Gifts of Imperfection*

Nowhere to hide

Peter betrays not only Jesus, but himself. He allows his fear and shame to override the truth that he is a follower and friend of Jesus. But onlookers see who he really is—in his manner of speaking, his presence at Caiaphas's house, and his unspoken love for and faith in Jesus.

Peter is not alone. We often sacrifice our identity as beloved children of God by words and actions that deny the depths of our faith, our trust in prayer, our hope in God's salvation. The disconnect between our inward faith and our outward lives distracts from our witness and denies our God-given gifts. God continues to call us beyond ourselves, however, to outward witness that reveals our inward faith.

After the resurrection, Christ empowers Peter to preach and teach for the sake of the world. Peter goes on to confess his fear and faith as he witnesses to what he has seen.

Prayer

Giver of faith, forgive us when fear and shame prevent us from proclaiming your love. Help us to share our inward faith through our words and acts of service. Amen.

March 28

Matthew 27:1-4a

When morning came, all the chief priests and the elders of the people conferred together against Jesus in order to bring about his death. They bound him, led him away, and handed him over to Pilate the governor. When Judas, his betrayer, saw that Jesus was condemned, he repented and brought back the thirty pieces of silver to the chief priests and the elders. He said, "I have sinned by betraying innocent blood."

To ponder

We Christians must be armed and expect every day to be under continuous attack. . . . At such times our only help and comfort is to run here and seize hold of the Lord's Prayer and speak to God from our heart, "Dear Father, you have commanded me to pray; let me not fall because of temptation." . . . Otherwise, if you attempt to help yourself by your own thoughts and resources, you will only make the matter worse and give the devil a wider opening. —Martin Luther, "The Large Catechism"

A collection of pieces

Judas gives in to the temptations of power and greed when he gives over his teacher and Lord for a huge sum of money. Given the same situation, we like to think we would resist temptation. Truth is, the forces that defy God, resist faith, and offer temptation surround all of us every day.

Judas's delight in receiving a large sum of money doesn't last long. When he sees the consequences of his actions, he is cut to the heart. The pieces of silver weigh on him. Keeping them isn't an option, even if he has to confess his sin before the religious leaders.

This public confession reveals Judas's desire to let go of the silver pieces and hang on to the pieces of life in Christ that will bring relief: the hope for mercy and forgiveness. We learn from Judas to confess our sin, knowing that we too can always turn back into the loving arms of Christ.

Prayer

God of mercy, deliver us from temptation and all that pulls us into self-centered living and sin. Give us courage to confess our sin. Strengthen us by your mercy and forgiveness, through Jesus Christ. Amen.

March 29 / Lent 5

Matthew 27:11-14

Now Jesus stood before the governor; and the governor asked him, "Are you the King of the Jews?" Jesus said, "You say so." But when he was accused by the chief priests and elders, he did not answer. Then Pilate said to him, "Do you not hear how many accusations they make against you?" But he gave him no answer, not even to a single charge, so that the governor was greatly amazed.

To ponder

We gathered around that table. And there was more singing and standing, and someone was putting a piece of fresh, crumbly bread in my hands, saying, "The body of Christ," and handing me the goblet of sweet wine, saying, "The blood of Christ," and then something outrageous and terrifying happened. Jesus happened to me. —Sara Miles, *Take This Bread*

Everything answers

Why is Pilate so amazed? Is it that Jesus makes no defense to save himself or offer more explanation? Is it that Jesus stands silent in this emotionally charged situation, when the outcome will be suffering and death? Or perhaps the governor knows on some level that Jesus is all that he is accused of being—the very King of the Jews, the Messiah, the Son of God.

Jesus doesn't need to give breath to proofs and explanations. He stands as the very presence of God in the flesh. Everything in the room stands in witness to the creative and awe-inspiring power of God who made all things. Every person in the room has been made by the same God who lives and breathes in the one who stands accused.

We all seek signs and proofs of the truth of God's salvation and grace, and yet the Creator's fingerprints are already on every aspect of the world, seen and unseen. Signs already surround us in water, bread, and wine—means of grace that show us God's presence.

Let us attune our ears to the deafening silence that testifies to the power and awe of God's presence.

Prayer

God of all, help us to pause and wonder with delight at all you have made. Open our hearts to see the evidence of your presence and salvation in all that surrounds us. Amen.

March 30

Matthew 27:15-18

Now at the festival the governor [Pilate] was accustomed to release a prisoner for the crowd, anyone whom they wanted. At that time they had a notorious prisoner, called Jesus Barabbas. So after they had gathered, Pilate said to them, "Whom do you want me to release for you, Jesus Barabbas or Jesus who is called the Messiah?" For he realized that it was out of jealousy that they had handed him over.

To ponder

The import of the commandment against killing is this: In the first place, we should not harm anyone. . . . In the second place, this commandment is violated not only when a person actually does evil, but also when he fails to do good to his neighbor, or, though he has the opportunity, fails to prevent, protect and save him from suffering bodily harm or injury. —Martin Luther, "The Large Catechism"

The momentum of sin

The train has left the station and the momentum is unstoppable. Unwilling to listen to Pilate's protests, the crowd condemns Jesus to death. Jealous of the authority they perceive in Jesus, those in power hand him over to death. The sin of the world propels all toward a gruesome execution.

The gift of the commandments shows the way for God's people to be in relationship with God and the community. There is no denying that the leaders and the crowd shatter these commands in calling for the death of Jesus. There is no escape from the brokenness of humanity. Sin propels Jesus to the cross and death.

Yet God's grace and mercy will be revealed in this brokenness. The shattered commandments make way for the power of resurrection and life. Christ's body will be sacrificed and broken at the hands of humanity, but the sin of the world that propels Jesus to the cross is not the final destination. In Christ, the momentum carries on into eternal life.

Prayer

God of life, give us the courage to acknowledge the depths of our brokenness, so that we may see the immeasurable mercy of your salvation through the death and resurrection of our Lord, Jesus Christ. Amen.

Matthew 27:20-23

Now the chief priests and the elders persuaded the crowds to ask for Barabbas and to have Jesus killed. The governor again said to them, "Which of the two do you want me to release for you?" And they said, "Barabbas." Pilate said to them, "Then what should I do with Jesus who is called the Messiah?" All of them said, "Let him be crucified!" Then he asked, "Why, what evil has he done?" But they shouted all the more, "Let him be crucified!"

To ponder

Life is not fair. The wrong people get sick and the wrong people get robbed and the wrong people get killed in wars and in accidents. . . . Our responding to life's unfairness with sympathy and with righteous indignation, God's compassion and God's anger

working through us, may be the surest proof of all of God's reality.
—Harold S. Kushner, *When Bad Things Happen to Good People*

Crucify the "why"

The crowd demands the death of Jesus. "Why?" Pilate asks. His question hangs in the air unanswered as the crowd, unfazed, continues its crucifixion chant.

Why does the crowd insist on the death of an innocent teacher? Like the relentless "why" questions of a young child, Pilate's question leaves us feeling unsettled and frustrated. The crowd at this point is caught in tension between the unfolding salvation story and their unsettling participation in that story. They seek salvation while they condemn the one who will bring it.

Jesus will resolve this lingering "why" question in his suffering and resurrection. The condemnation of the crowd nails Jesus to the cross, but God's compassion transforms that condemnation into grace and mercy. We linger at the cusp between death and life, on the edge of the water that drowns and brings life in baptism. We linger with the "why" question, drawn into the unfolding story that will have sin and grace meet to bring the love of God.

Prayer

God of mercy, as Jesus carries our sin to the cross, silence our questions and doubts. Inspire us to humbly confess our sins and wait for signs of your salvation. Strengthen us with the love and compassion of Christ, who died for us. Amen.

Matthew 27:27-29, 31

Then the soldiers of the governor took Jesus into the governor's headquarters, and they gathered the whole cohort around him. They stripped him and put a scarlet robe on him, and after twisting some thorns into a crown, they put it on his head. They put a reed in his right hand and knelt before him and mocked him, saying, "Hail, King of the Jews!" . . . After mocking him, they stripped him of the robe and put his own clothes on him. Then they led him away to crucify him.

To ponder

O sacred head, now wounded, with grief and shame weighed down, now scornfully surrounded with thorns, thine only crown; O sacred head, what glory, what bliss till now was thine!

Yet, though despised and gory, I joy to call thee mine.
—Paul Gerhardt, "O sacred head, now wounded," ELW 351, st. 1

Suffering and love

The soldiers don't know the irony of their actions. The makeshift reed scepter and crown of thorns are but shadows of the royal accoutrements, usually made of precious metals and stones, of an earthly king. The soldiers unwittingly reveal the paradoxical truth of Jesus' reign. Humiliation makes way for glory. Suffering makes way for healing. Death makes way for life.

Words fail at times when suffering and love meet. It is difficult even to look upon scenes of suffering. Sometimes we quickly look away in discomfort and disgust, but other times we stare and gawk, unable to tear our eyes away. When a dear loved one is the victim, our insides turn and we can feel the physical and emotional pain.

We watch and wait as this story unfolds, wrestling with the suffering and abuse inflicted on Jesus. In the horror of it all, the compassion and mercy of God become real. The meeting place of suffering and love is revealed, and even now we see the truth of Jesus' reign of forgiveness and mercy.

Prayer

God of mercy and love, the suffering of Jesus reveals the lengths you will go to meet us in our pain and heartache. Strengthen us in times of trial, and show us your mercy. Amen.

April 2

Matthew 27:32-34

As they went out, they came upon a man from Cyrene named Simon; they compelled this man to carry his cross. And when they came to a place called Golgotha (which means Place of a Skull), they offered him wine to drink, mixed with gall; but when he tasted it, he would not drink it.

To ponder

The turbulence of Fonteyn's personal life revealed her gracefulness as a core value, not just an aspect of performance. The defining characteristic of her brand of grace was serenity . . . [and] her workmanlike ability to make the best of things, whether it was the limited limberness of her body or her marriage. In doing so, she transcended her difficulties. . . . Within many a graceful person—dancer, athlete, whomever—beats a large and uncomplaining heart. —Sarah L. Kaufman, *The Art of Grace*

Open our hearts

The power of empathy is inspiring. There is a grace that appears in those who show great kindness and resilience when facing difficult circumstances. These are people with "large and uncomplaining hearts." Often we discover these qualities shining brightly among those with the least wealth and privilege.

Simon of Cyrene is an elusive figure who would be unknown to us if he had not carried the cross of Jesus. We do not condone the use of force that compelled him to bear this burden. And yet we may find our own "brand of grace" as we allow the Holy Spirit to open our hearts to the burdens of others and the needs of our broken world. This kind of spiritual gift can be nurtured in our hearts and minds as we seek to live faithfully in the wondrous love of Christ.

Prayer

By your grace, O God, show us again the great mysteries of how we encounter you through giving, serving, and patiently accompanying those who need us to be present. Amen.

Matthew 27:35-37

And when they had crucified [Jesus], they divided his clothes among themselves by casting lots; then they sat down there and kept watch over him. Over his head they put the charge against him, which read, "This is Jesus, the King of the Jews."

To ponder

Everything we do is about winning something or measuring one person against another or garnering goods in great quantity, not because we need them but in order that others can't have them. We make life one great competition, a win-lose situation, a measuring stick by which we parade our value to others and, saddest of all, use those same things to convince ourselves of our own value. As if what we get . . . [is] any indicator at all of what is at the soul of us internally. —Joan Chittister, *The Way of the Cross*

True riches

During a retreat at the Taizé compound in France, a young American shared a remarkable discovery. He said: "Back home, surrounded by all my possessions, I often feel uncertain about many things. Here, with only a backpack, in the company of people who want to be together in the presence of God, I feel rich in every way. With the prayers, the songs, the silence, and the honest conversations about faith and life, I have everything I need."

The wondrous love of God invites us to live with freedom from the systems that foster greed, selfish living, and domination. The soldiers who mock Jesus find a way to take possession of his clothes—but they cannot break his spirit. As the apostle Paul writes, "We are treated as impostors, and yet are true; . . . as dying, and see—we are alive; . . . as poor, yet making many rich; as having nothing, and yet possessing everything" (2 Corinthians 6:8-10).

Celebrate the richness of the new life that is yours because Jesus' death overcomes the power of sin. His sovereign rule will free you from greed, excess, and the futility of seeking happiness in the things you possess.

Prayer

Giver of every perfect gift, thank you for filling my life with true riches that cannot be taken away. Amen.

Matthew 27:38-40

Then two bandits were crucified with him, one on his right and one on his left. Those who passed by derided him, shaking their heads and saying, "You who would destroy the temple and build it in three days, save yourself! If you are the Son of God, come down from the cross."

To ponder

We need people—and sometimes need to be people—who are willing to go to extremes. But we should also hope to be among those people who can find their way around the middle ground ... recognizing what rich territory may be found there. —Marilyn McEntyre, *Make a List*

Holy ground

On each side of Jesus on the cross is a bandit, a convicted criminal condemned to die the cruel death of crucifixion. Based on the circumstances, passersby jump to the conclusion that Jesus is also guilty, a fraud claiming to be God's Son.

When the Son of God refuses to come down from the cross, we begin to suspect that there is more going on here than meets the eye. The ground that holds the cross is sacred, holy, and precious. Jesus' suffering and death reveal a gracious alternative to life defined and ruled by hasty and superficial assumptions that divide people into winners and losers, insiders and outsiders, and "us" versus "them."

Jesus honors the "rich territory" that is free from these callous judgments. He who was crucified and died is with all who suffer from violence, abuse, and injustice. He is with all who work to change systems that perpetuate cycles of poverty and marginalization. He is with all who stand in the "middle ground" to mediate between opposing sides. Jesus' suffering and death will reveal God's power to bring about justice, transformation, and a new creation for all.

Prayer

Holy One, your justice mirrors your grace. Free me from shallow judgments. Use me in bringing about your new creation. Amen.

Matthew 27:41-44

The chief priests also, along with the scribes and elders, were mocking him, saying, "He saved others; he cannot save himself. He is the King of Israel; let him come down from the cross now, and we will believe in him. He trusts in God; let God deliver him now, if he wants to; for he said, 'I am God's Son.'" The bandits who were crucified with him also taunted him in the same way.

To ponder

Her mother pulled [Ifemelu's] ear, an almost gentle tug, as though reluctant to cause real pain. . . . She pulled it twice, once and then again to emphasize her words. "The devil is using you. You have to pray about this. Do not judge. Leave the judging to God!"
—Chimamanda Ngozi Adichie, *Americanah*

The only judgment that matters

A small Nigerian congregation is rumored to have ties to dirty money. A young woman named Ifemelu has spoken hastily, adding to the climate of suspicion. Her mother pleads with her to not be so quick to judge others.

Throughout his ministry, Jesus was the subject of many rumors. Even now as he suffers on the cross, pouring out the power of his redeeming love, he is mocked and judged. Those who publicly shame him cannot believe he is the Son of God.

Our spirits cringe as we read this scripture text because we know Jesus doesn't deserve this humiliation. But we also know he will overcome the powers of sin, death, and even the demonic ones. So we watch and pray, grateful that this wondrous love is freely offered to strengthen us when we ourselves are judged unfairly by the world. The only judgment that matters belongs to our God of justice, truth, and liberation.

Prayer

Gracious God, free us from the urge to speak with haste, offending those we fail to fully understand. Let our words always honor your wondrous love. Amen.

April 6

Matthew 27:45-46, 50

From noon on, darkness came over the whole land until three in the afternoon. And about three o'clock Jesus cried with a loud voice, "Eli, Eli, lema sabachthani?" that is, "My God, my God, why have you forsaken me?" . . . Then Jesus cried again with a loud voice and breathed his last.

To ponder

As Reverend Deal moved into his sermon, the hands of the women unfolded like pairs of raven's wings and flew high above their hats in the air. . . . Then they left their pews. For with some emotions one has to stand. They spoke, for they were full and needed to say. They swayed, for the rivulets of grief or of ecstasy must be rocked. And when they thought of all that life and death locked into that little closed coffin, they danced and screamed, not to protest God's will but to acknowledge it. —Toni Morrison, *Sula*

Jesus cried out

Many of us find it difficult to deal with the death of someone close to us, whether the transition from this life is surprisingly peaceful, extraordinarily difficult, or something in between. We struggle with the impact of the loss and the truth of our own mortality. We struggle to deal with emotions that make us and those around us uncomfortable and even afraid.

In crying out on the cross, Jesus makes room in the life of his church for all of us who need to cry out and express our grief with shouting and moaning and groaning, with swaying and rocking and dancing. He cries out for all who feel abandoned, and for all facing their own death or the death of a loved one.

Jesus cries out to God with the opening words of Psalm 22. This psalm also says: "In you our ancestors trusted; they trusted, and you delivered them. To you they cried, and were saved; in you they trusted, and were not put to shame" (vv. 4-5). We too can cry out to God, knowing that we will be heard.

Prayer

Merciful God, whenever grief surrounds us you graciously draw near. We give thanks for such wondrous love. Let all that is within us bless your holy name. Amen.

Matthew 27:51-52

At that moment the curtain of the temple was torn in two, from top to bottom. The earth shook, and the rocks were split. The tombs also were opened, and many bodies of the saints who had fallen asleep were raised.

To ponder

Paul confronted death—examined it, wrestled with it, accepted it—as a physician and a patient. He wanted to help people understand death and face their mortality. . . . Of course, he did more than just describe the terrain. He traversed it bravely. —Lucy Kalanithi, in *When Breath Becomes Air*

And when from death I'm free

A universal metaphor for spiritual growth is finding your way, discovering the path, walking the road. Early followers of Jesus were called the people of The Way, indicating that they were finding purpose and direction as they were being led by the Holy Spirit. As we walk this mysterious road, the way may at times seem completely mundane; at other times it may suddenly be illuminated by leaps of faith and transcendent experiences of amazing grace.

What lies up ahead? For the faithful, this is best described as a world immersed in the promises of God's wondrous love. Though this love may seem hidden as we encounter Jesus' suffering and death, God is with us always—even beyond death. As if to announce that promise in no uncertain terms, Matthew 27 tells of earthquakes shaking open tombs and of saints being raised. My, what a road this is! The way of Jesus brings us to the grandeur of life restored and transformed.

Prayer

God of restoration and transformation, my soul sings with joy unspeakable: What wondrous love is this! And when from death I'm free, I'll sing on. And when from death I'm free, I'll sing God's love for me, and through eternity I'll sing on. Amen. (adapted from "What wondrous love is this"; ELW 666, st. 4)

April 8

Matthew 27:54

Now when the centurion and those with him, who were keeping watch over Jesus, saw the earthquake and what took place, they were terrified and said, "Truly this man was God's Son!"

To ponder

"During the other protests, I watched. And talked. So now I wanna do something."

"Who said talking isn't doing something?" she says. "It's more productive than silence. Remember what I told you about your voice?"

"You said it's my biggest weapon."

"And I meant that."

—Angie Thomas, *The Hate U Give*

Lift every voice

Up to this point in Matthew's gospel the centurion (an officer in the Roman army) and the men under his command have obeyed orders and done what is expected of them. At Pilate's headquarters soldiers put a robe and a crown of thorns on Jesus and mocked him as "King of the Jews," then led him away to Golgotha. They cast lots for his clothes as he was crucified. They carried out the execution of Jesus, and no riot erupted. They have done their job.

But now the earth shakes, tombs are abandoned, and rocks split in two. Surprising events, but even more surprising is the reaction of the centurion and soldiers to this divine disruption: *This man was God's Son!*

The centurion and his companions are soldiers, not prophets, but their testimony matters. It becomes part of the good news God calls us to tell the world. You have heard this good news, so lift your voice, even if you think you are the most unlikely person to do so. Share the holy gospel. Become part of the story of what God has done through Jesus Christ, because in the world of faith, hope, and wondrous love, every voice matters.

Prayer

Holy One, speak to us, that we may speak in living echoes of your tone. Amen. (adapted from "Lord, speak to us, that we may speak," by Frances R. Havergal, ELW 676, st. 1)

April 9 / Maundy Thursday

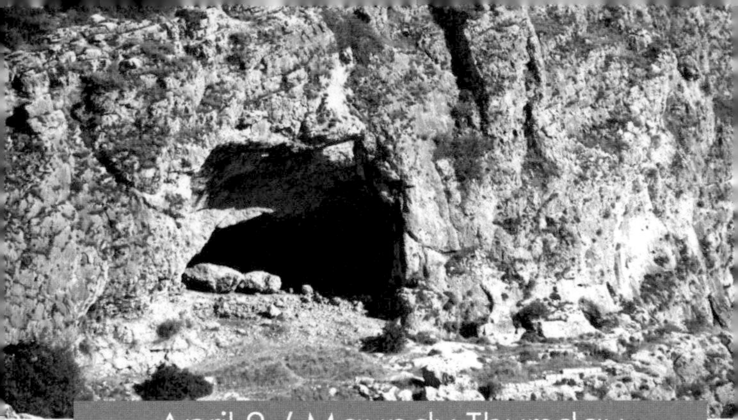

Matthew 27:57-61

When it was evening, there came a rich man from Arimathea, named Joseph, who was also a disciple of Jesus. He went to Pilate and asked for the body of Jesus; then Pilate ordered it to be given to him. So Joseph took the body and wrapped it in a clean linen cloth and laid it in his own new tomb, which he had hewn in the rock. He then rolled a great stone to the door of the tomb and went away. Mary Magdalene and the other Mary were there, sitting opposite the tomb.

To ponder

By your deep expiring groan, by the sad sepulchral stone,
by the vault whose dark abode held in vain the rising God,
oh, from earth to heav'n restored, mighty, re-ascended Lord,

bending from your throne on high, hear our penitential cry!
—Robert Grant, "Savior, when in dust to you," ELW 601, st. 4

Even the stones will shout

At this point in Matthew's gospel all hope is gone. Jesus has been arrested, put on trial, and crucified. Now he is dead. Buried in a tomb chiseled out of rock. A "sad sepulchral stone" seals the tomb. To the world's eye, this stone also seals his fate. The misguided Messiah's ministry has ended. The prophet is silenced. The charade is over.

It seems odd to describe a silent, inanimate stone as "sad." But in Luke, when some Pharisees begged Jesus to tell his disciples to stop shouting their hosannas, Jesus said, "If these were silent, the stones would shout out" (19:40). It seems that even stones can't stay quiet about Jesus.

The one who lies in the tomb behind the stone is the one who was present at creation when stones were first formed. Stones scattered beneath his feet as he made his way to the cross. Very soon, behind this stone blocking the tomb's entrance, God will raise Jesus from death and turn all creation's longing into joy. Perhaps even the stones will shout!

Prayer

Lord Jesus, open our lips, that we may join the stones and all creation in singing your praise. You alone have given your life for the love of all people. And you alone are risen from the dead. Amen.

April 10 / Good Friday

Matthew 27:62-65

The chief priests and the Pharisees gathered before Pilate and said, "Sir, we remember what that impostor said while he was still alive, 'After three days I will rise again.' Therefore command the tomb to be made secure until the third day; otherwise his disciples may go and steal him away, and tell the people, 'He has been raised from the dead,' and the last deception would be worse than the first." Pilate said to them, "You have a guard of soldiers; go, make it as secure as you can."

To ponder

What wondrous love is this, O my soul, O my soul!
What wondrous love is this, O my soul!
What wondrous love is this that caused the Lord of bliss

to bear the dreadful curse for my soul, for my soul,
to bear the dreadful curse for my soul?
—"What wondrous love is this," ELW 666, st. 1

What wondrous love is this?

"The last deception would be worse than the first." In the minds of the chief priests and Pharisees, just what is the first deception—that Jesus was able to rally a following? Are they jealous of Jesus' popularity? Do they fear a possible uprising? Or are the chief priests, Pharisees, Pilate—and all the people who surround Jesus—unable to come to terms with his wondrous love?

Political leaders tend to rely on power, maneuvering, and political clout. In their minds, Jesus' first deception might be "love wins." But as the chief priests and Pharisees continue to plan and plot, we are just one resurrected breath away from the truth.

Fast-forward two thousand years. Many people still rely on power and political clout to make their way in the world. It is up to the baptized community of the Crucified One to both carry and live his message: Love wins.

What wondrous love is this, O my soul? It is the wondrous love of Jesus who is slumbering in the tomb and about to come to life forever.

Prayer

Gracious, merciful, living God, we offer you our thanks and praise for the greatest love the world has ever seen or known. Help us to bring your wondrous love into the world. Amen.

Matthew 28:1-8

As the first day of the week was dawning, Mary Magdalene and the other Mary went to see the tomb. And suddenly there was a great earthquake; for an angel of the Lord, descending from heaven, came and rolled back the stone and sat on it. His appearance was like lightning, and his clothing white as snow. For fear of him the guards shook and became like dead men. But the angel said to the women, "Do not be afraid; I know that you are looking for Jesus who was crucified. He is not here; for he has been raised, as he said. Come, see the place where he lay. Then go quickly and tell his disciples, 'He has been raised from the dead, and indeed he is going ahead of you to Galilee; there you will see him.' This is my message for you." So they left the tomb quickly with fear and great joy, and ran to tell his disciples.

To ponder

Something strange is happening—there is a great silence on earth today, a great silence and stillness. The whole earth keeps silence because the King is asleep. God has died in the flesh and hell trembles with fear. —Epiphanius of Cyprus, "From an Ancient Homily"

Go and tell

This is a day like no other. This is the day when God slumbers in the tomb. And as this day of days draws to a close and Easter morning dawns, all creation holds its breath to see what will happen next. What will God do with a crucified Jesus?

"Do not be afraid," an angel says to women at the tomb at daybreak. It makes sense that the women might tremble in fear. Even the earth is quaking, according to Matthew. We fear things that are unfamiliar, and nothing is as unfamiliar as this—an angelic announcement about a person raised from the dead!

What will we do with a resurrected Jesus? The women at the tomb were not held back by fear. Like them, we can run to tell the news, sharing Christ's wondrous love with the world as we go. He is risen! Alleluia!

Prayer

Risen Lord Jesus, you have taken away the sting of death. Please take away our fear. Empower us to live out our baptism and to serve you boldly in the world. Amen.

Notes

Welcome: North American folk hymn, 19th cent., "What wondrous love is this," ELW 666, st. 1. **February 26:** Robert Grant, "Savior, when in dust to you," ELW 601, st. 1. **February 27:** Maximus of Turin, "Sermo 100" ("de Sancta Epiphania"), 1.3. *In Eco-Reformation: Grace and Hope for a Planet in Peril*, Lisa E. Dahill and James B. Martin-Schramm, eds. (Eugene, OR: Cascade Books, 2016), 169–170. **February 29:** William Williams, "Guide me ever, great Redeemer," ELW 618, st. 1. **March 2:** "Savior, when in dust to you," ELW 601, st. 2. **March 3:** Alfred North Whitehead, *Modes of Thought* (New York: The Free Press, 1968). **March 4:** William H. Willimon, *Undone by Easter: Keeping Preaching Fresh* (Nashville: Abingdon, 2009), 40. **March 5:** Valentin Lebedev, July 31, 1982, in Frank White, *The Overview Effect: Space Exploration and Human Evolution* (Boston: Houghton Mifflin, 1987), 231. **March 6:** Sara Miles, *Jesus Freak: Feeding, Healing, Raising the Dead* (San Francisco: Jossey-Bass, 2010), 24. **March 7:** Henri Nouwen, *Here and Now: Living in the Spirit* (New York: Crossroad, 1994), 60, 62. **March 8:** Kathleen Norris, *Amazing Grace: A Vocabulary of Faith* (New York: Riverhead, 1998), 225. **March 9:** Barbara Brown Taylor, *Mixed Blessings* (Cambridge, MA: Cowley, 1998), 102. **March 10:** Julian of Norwich, in Veronica Mary Rolf, *An Explorer's Guide to Julian of Norwich* (Downers Grove, IL: IVP Academic, 2018), 144. **March 11:** Donald F. Glut, *Star Wars: The Empire Strikes Back* (New York: Ballantine Books, 1980), 137. **March 12:** *ELW*, 264. **March 13:** Laura Sobiech, *Fly a Little Higher: How God Answered a Mom's Small Prayer in a Big Way* (Nashville: Thomas Nelson, 2014), 173. **March 14:** Diane Ackerman, *A Natural History of the Senses* (New York: Vintage Books, 1995), 79. **March 15:** Michelle Alexander, *The New Jim Crow: Mass Incarceration in the Age of Colorblindness* (New York: The New Press, 2012), 166. **March 16:** Colby Martin, *Unclobber: Rethinking Our Misuse of the Bible on Homosexuality* (Louisville: Westminster John Knox Press, 2016), 143. **March 17:** Bradley Trevor Greive, *Every Day Is Christmas: Living the Holiday Spirit throughout the Year without Damaging Your Health or Driving Everyone Crazy* (Kansas City, MO: Andrews McMeel, 2011), 53. **March 18:** Eugene H. Peterson, *A Long Obedience in the Same Direction: Discipleship in an Instant Society* (Downers Grove, IL: InterVarsity Press, 2012), 90. **March 19:** Martin Luther, "The Large Catechism," Book of Concord: *The Confessions of the Evangelical Lutheran Church*, Robert Kolb and Timothy J. Wengert, eds. (Minneapolis: Fortress Press, 2000), 478–479. **March 20:** Robert Robinson, "Come, thou Fount of every blessing," ELW 807, st. 3. **March 21:** Michael Gerson, "I was hospitalized for depression: Faith helped me remember how to live," *Washington Post*, February 18, 2019. **March 22:** "What wondrous love is this," ELW 666, st. 2. **March 23:** Henry Chadwick, *The Early Church* (London: Penguin Books, 1993), 261–262. **March 24:** Tish Harrison Warren, *The Liturgy of the Ordinary* (Downers Grove, IL: IVP Books, 2016), 112–113. **March 25:** Anne Lamott, *Hallelujah Anyway: Rediscovering Mercy* (New York: Riverhead Books, 2017), 62–63. **March 26:** C. S. Lewis, *The Lion, the Witch, and the Wardrobe* (New York: Macmillan, 1950), 155. **March 27:** Brené Brown, *The Gifts of Imperfection: Let Go of Who You Think You're Supposed to Be and Embrace Who You Are* (Center City, MN: Hazelden, 2010), 103. **March 28:** Martin Luther, "The Large Catechism," *The Book of Concord*, 455. **March 29:** Sara Miles, *Take This Bread: The Spiritual Memoir of a Twenty-First-Century Christian* (New York: Ballantine Books, 2008), 58. **March 30:** Martin Luther, "The Large Catechism," *The Book of Concord*, 390–391. **March 31:** Harold S. Kushner, *When Bad Things Happen to Good People* (New York: Anchor Books, 2007), 155–156. **April 1:** Paul Gerhardt, "O sacred head, now wounded," ELW 351, st. 1. **April 2:** Sarah L. Kaufman, *The Art of Grace: On Moving Well through Life* (New York: W. W. Norton & Company, Inc., 2016), 154–155. **April 3:** Joan Chittister, *The Way of the Cross: The Path to New Life* (New York: Orbis Books), 31. **April 4:** Marilyn McEntyre, *Make a List* (Grand Rapids, MI: Wm. B. Eerdmans, 2018), 50–52. **April 5:** Chimamanda Ngozi Adichie, *Americanah* (New York: Anchor Books, 2013), 63. **April 6:** Toni Morrison, *Sula* (New York: Alfred A. Knopf, 1973), 65–66. **April 7:** Lucy Kalanithi, Epilogue, in Paul Kalanithi, *When Breath Becomes Air* (New York: Random House, 2016), 215. Prayer adapted from "What wondrous love is this," ELW 676, st. 4. **April 8:** Angie Thomas, *The Hate U Give* (New York: Balzer + Bray, 2017), 410. Prayer adapted from Frances R. Havergal, "Lord, speak to us, that we may speak," ELW 676, st. 1. **April 9:** "Savior, when in dust to you," ELW 601, st. 4. **April 10:** "What wondrous love is this," ELW 666, st. 1. **April 11:** Epiphanius of Cyprus, "From an Ancient Homily," in *Triduum Sourcebook* (Chicago: Liturgy Training Publications, 2007), 65.